A Selection of Odes by

Pessoa by Me Collection

Volume 3

Cover: Photo by Cottonbro Studio in pexel.com

Source for text in Portuguese: http://arquivopessoa.net/

A Selection of Odes by Ricardo Reis

as written

by Fernando Pessoa

Bilingual Edition

Selected and Translated

by Erick Messias 2023 ©

Introducing Pessoa by Me   6
Introducing Ricardo Reis   7
Para ser grande, sê inteiro   13
To be great, be whole   14
Segue o teu destino   15
Follow your destiny   16
Nada fica de nada. Nada somos.   21
Nothing is left of nothing. We are nothing.   22
Quer pouco: terás tudo.   23
Want little: you'll have everything.   24
Não só quem nos odeia ou nos inveja   25
Not only those who hate or envy us   26
Não tenhas nada nas mãos   27
Don't hold anything in your hands   28
Cada um cumpre o destino que lhe cumpre.   31
Everyone fulfills their own destiny   32
Cada coisa a seu tempo tem seu tempo.   33
Each thing on its own time has its own time.   34
Tornar-te-ás só quem tu sempre foste.   39
You'll become just who you've always been.   40
Cada dia sem gozo não foi teu   41
Every day without enjoyment wasn't yours   42
Negue-me tudo a sorte, menos vê-la,   43
Deny me anything, Luck   44
No breve número de doze meses   45
In the low number of twelve months   46

Quero ignorado, e calmo 47

I want ignored, and calm 48

Colhe o dia, porque és ele. 49

Harvest the day, because you are it 50

Amo o que vejo 51

I love what I see 52

Estás só. Ninguém o sabe. 53

You are alone. Nobody knows. 54

Tenho Mais Almas que Uma 55

I have more than one soul 56

Vem sentar-te comigo, Lídia, à beira do rio. 59

Come and sit with me, Lidia, by the river. 60

Ouvi contar que outrora, quando a Pérsia 65

I've heard that once upon a time, when Persia 66

Breve o dia, breve o ano, breve tudo. 79

Short the day, short the year, short everything. 80

Mestre, são plácidas 81

Master, they are placid 82

Coroai-me de rosas, 89

Crown me with roses, 90

About the authors: Fernando Pessoa - One and Many - by ChatGPT 92

About the Authors: Ricardo Reis 94

About this translation 96

Introducing Pessoa by Me

Something surprised me when I first read or heard about Fernando Pessoa while in America. The great poet was known mostly by his prose volume known as The Book of Disquiet. The great poems cited included "Salutation to Walt Whitman" and "Maritime Ode."

Where was the poet and the poets, Caeiro, Campos and Reis? And where were lines such as "the poet is a sham" or "I am nothing, I will never be but nothing. I can't wish but to be nothing. Aside from this, I have in me every dream in the world" or "To be great, be whole" or "To think of God is to disobey God," - lines that I could find in my memory after all those years?

I then realized that to bring the Pessoa that populated my adolescence imagination I would have to look for those poems myself and thus this collection was created.

This is not an academic exercise, this is not professional translation, this is a work of love and *Saudade*. This is a way to introduce a Pessoa I met and left deep marks in my existence to my American children and friends. This is a way to collect the poems I encountered as an adolescent in Fortaleza in the 1990s and that have been with me since.

Erick Leite Maia de Messias

Introducing Ricardo Reis

A Classic Poet speaking for Epicureans, Stoics, and Buddhists.

The poet Fernando Pessoa was many poets in one - having written under many persona throughout his life. Three of these - what he called heteronyms to differentiate from mere pseudonyms - are "full fledged" complete poets: Alberto Caeiro, Alvaro de Campos and Ricardo Reis . Of these three Ricardo Reis is the most formally educated, philosophical and possibly the more melancholic of the group.

For these heteronyms Pessoa would create a specific biography. According to this biography, Ricardo Reis was born in 1887 in the city of Porto, Portugal. He had a Jesuit education, studied medicine, and migrated to Brazil in 1919 in part due to his monarchist inclinations - Portugal became a republic in 1910. His Jesuit education gave him a depth of knowledge in ancient - Greek and Latin - traditions and literature. Pessoa describes Reis as a "pagan" and a "purist".

Given this background, it is not surprising that Ricardo Rei's poetry from a philosophical perspective leans towards two Ancient schools: Epicureanism and Stoicism. From Epicureanism Reis brings in the idea of Joy repeated in poems like:

Every day without enjoyment wasn't yours

You only lasted in it. How long you live

Without enjoying it, you're not living.

From Stoicism Reis brings the idea of living "placidly" which can be interpreted as the "ataraxia" idea of the Stoics:

To the night that comes in doesn't belong, Lydia,

The same ardor that the day asked of us.

Let us placidly love

Our uncertain life.

From the Stoics you can also identify the resignation facing the world and facing death, as in:

Nothing is left of nothing. We are nothing.

A little in the sun and the air so we lag behind

The unbreathable darkness that weighs us down

The damp earth imposed on us,

Postponed corpses that procreate.

In one poem he merges the two themes and calls himself a "stoic without hardness."

Deny me anything, Luck, but to see her,

That I, 'stoic without hardness,

In the engraved sentence of Fate

want to enjoy letters.

Throughout these philosophical themes one can also identify the classic education and style of Ricardo Reis in his frequent reference to the Olympic gods.

But placidly

Imitate Olympus

In your heart.

Gods are gods

Because they don't think.

One philosophical perspective not frequently mentioned when discussing Ricardo Reis' odes is Buddhism. One of the "four noble truths" of Buddhism is:

Suffering is caused by craving.

In Ricardo Reis we find time and again the notion that it is key to life is "not to want", as in:

But to those who expect nothing

Everything that comes is grateful.

And again in:

Want little: you will have everything.

Want nothing: you will be free.

Furthermore in several Odes we see the Buddhist theme of impermanence as in:

Nothing is left of nothing. We are nothing.

A little in the sun and the air so we lag behind

The unbreathable darkness that weighs us down

The damp earth imposed on us,

Postponed corpses that procreate.

Examining Reis' poetry from these different philosophical perspectives can enrich the reading in two ways: first, it gives the reader a complex philosophical background on which to refer back on the ideas posed by each poem; second, it makes one realize how contemporary Pessoa/Reis can be today when we are ready to embrace a multicultural, multilingual and multi-tradition existence. In that sense reading Pessoa/Reis is as much enriching today as it was one hundred years ago when these verses were penned.

Finally, regardless of the reader's philosophical inclinations, the sheer beauty of these lines are worth your time and your attention - even if today we live with so little time and so short attention spans.

I hope you enjoy reading these poems and odes as much as I did in selecting and translating them.

Erick Messias

Saint Louis, MO

September 2023

Para ser grande, sê inteiro

Para ser grande, sê inteiro:

Nada teu exagera ou exclui.

Sê todo em cada coisa.

Põe quanto és no mínimo que fazes.

Assim em cada lago a lua toda

Brilha, porque alta vive.

To be great, be whole

To be great, be whole:

Nothing in you is too much or too little.

Be all in at every turn.

Put all that you are in the least you do.

So in every lake the whole moon shines,

because it stands high.

Segue o teu destino

Segue o teu destino,

Rega as tuas plantas,

Ama as tuas rosas.

O resto é a sombra

De árvores alheias.

A realidade

Sempre é mais ou menos

Do que nós queremos.

Só nós somos sempre

Iguais a nós-próprios.

Follow your destiny

Follow your destiny,

Water your plants,

Love your roses.

The rest is the shadow

Of other people's trees.

Reality

Is always more or less

What we want.

Only we are always

The same as ourselves.

Suave é viver só.

Grande e nobre é sempre

Viver simplesmente.

Deixa a dor nas aras

Como ex-voto aos deuses.

Vê de longe a vida.

Nunca a interrogues.

Ela nada pode

Dizer-te. A resposta

Está além dos deuses.

Gentle is to live alone.

Great and noble is always

To live simply.

Leave pain in the air

As an offering to the gods.

Look at life from afar.

Never question it.

It can

Tell you nothing. The answer

Is beyond the gods.

Mas serenamente

Imita o Olimpo

No teu coração.

Os deuses são deuses

Porque não se pensam.

But placidly

Imitate Olympus

In your heart.

Gods are gods

Because they don't think about themselves. .

Nada fica de nada. Nada somos.

Nada fica de nada. Nada somos.

Um pouco ao sol e ao ar nos atrasamos

Da irrespirável treva que nos pese

    Da húmida terra imposta,

Cadáveres adiados que procriam.

Leis feitas, estátuas vistas, odes findas —

Tudo tem cova sua. Se nós, carnes

A que um íntimo sol dá sangue, temos

    Poente, porque não elas?

Somos contos contando contos, nada

Nothing is left of nothing. We are nothing.

Nothing is left of nothing. We are nothing.

A little in the sun and the air so we lag behind

The unbreathable darkness that weighs us down

The damp earth imposed on us,

Postponed corpses that procreate.

Laws made, statues seen, odes completed -

Everything has its own grave. If we, flesh

To which an intimate sun gives blood, have the sunset

    Why not them?

We are tales telling tales, nothing

Quer pouco: terás tudo.

Quer pouco: terás tudo.

Quer nada: serás livre.

O mesmo amor que tenham

Por nós, quer-nos, oprime-nos.

Want little: you'll have everything.

Want little: you will have everything.

Want nothing: you will be free.

The same love they have

for us, hunts us, oppresses us.

Não só quem nos odeia ou nos inveja

Não só quem nos odeia ou nos inveja

Nos limita e oprime; quem nos ama

Não menos nos limita.

Que os deuses me concedam que, despido

De afectos, tenha a fria liberdade

Dos píncaros sem nada.

Quem quer pouco, tem tudo; quem quer nada

É livre; quem não tem, e não deseja,

Homem, é igual aos deuses.

Not only those who hate or envy us

Not only those who hate or envy us

Limits and oppresses us; those who love us

Limits us no less.

May the gods grant that, stripped bare

Of affections, I may have the cold freedom

Of the summits with nothing.

He who wants little has everything;

he who wants nothing is free;

He who doesn't have, doesn't want,

Man, is equal to the gods.

Não tenhas nada nas mãos

Não tenhas nada nas mãos

Nem uma memória na alma,

Que quando te puserem

Nas mãos o óbolo último,

Ao abrirem-te as mãos

Nada te cairá.

Que trono te querem dar

Que Átropos to não tire?

Don't hold anything in your hands

Hold nothing in your hands

Nor a memory in your soul,

So when they come to put

In your hands the last coin,

As they open your hands

Nothing will fall out.

What throne will they give you

That Atropos [1] won't take from you?

---

[1] Atropos, in Greek mythology, one of the three Fates, the others being Clotho and Lachesis. Atropos's name (meaning "unalterable" or "inflexible") indicates her function, that of rendering the decisions of her sisters irreversible or immutable. Atropos is most frequently represented with

Que louros que não fanem

Nos arbítrios de Minos?

Que horas que te não tornem

Da estatura da sombra

Que serás quando fores

Na noite e ao fim da estrada.

Colhe as flores mas larga-as,

Das mãos mal as olhaste.

Senta-te ao sol. Abdica

E sê rei de ti próprio.

---

scales, a sundial, or a cutting instrument, described by John
Milton in Lycidas as the "abhorred shears" with which she
"slits the thinspun life." - from Britannica

What laurels not to fan

In the will of Minos?

What hours do not turn you

Into the stature of a shadow

That you will be when you go

Into the night and at the end of the road.

Pick flowers but let them go from your hands,

You've barely looked at them.

Sit in the sun. Abdicate

And be king of yourself.

Cada um cumpre o destino que lhe cumpre.

Cada um cumpre o destino que lhe cumpre.

E deseja o destino que deseja;

     Nem cumpre o que deseja,

     Nem deseja o que cumpre.

Como as pedras na orla dos canteiros

O Fado nos dispõe, e ali ficamos;

     Que a Sorte nos fez postos

     Onde houvemos de sê-lo.

Não tenhamos melhor conhecimento

Do que nos coube que de que nos coube.

     Cumpramos o que somos.

     Nada mais nos é dado.

Everyone fulfills their own destiny

Everyone fulfills their own destiny.

And desires the destiny they desire;

      Neither fulfilling what desires,

      Nor desiring what fulfills.

Like stones at the edge of flower beds

Fate disposes us, and there we stay;

      Fortune has placed us

      Where we should be.

Let us have no better knowledge

Of what has befallen us than of what befalls us.

      Let us fulfill what we are.

      Nothing more is given to us.

Cada coisa a seu tempo tem seu tempo.

Cada coisa a seu tempo tem seu tempo.

Não florescem no Inverno os arvoredos,

Nem pela Primavera

Têm branco frio os campos.

À noite, que entra, não pertence, Lídia,

O mesmo ardor que o dia nos pedia.

Com mais sossego amemos

A nossa incerta vida.

Each thing on its own time has its own time.

Each thing on its time has its own time.

Trees don't bloom in winter,

Nor in spring

The fields are cold white.

To the night that comes in doesn't belong, Lydia,

The same ardor that the day asked of us.

Let us placidly love

Our uncertain life.

À lareira, cansados não da obra

Mas porque a hora é a hora dos cansaços,

Não puxemos a voz

Acima de um segredo,

E casuais, interrompidas sejam

Nossas palavras de reminiscência

(Não para mais nos serve

A negra ida do sol).

Pouco a pouco o passado recordemos

E as histórias contadas no passado

Agora duas vezes

Histórias, que nos falem

By the fire, tired not of the work

But because the hour is the hour of being tired,

Let's not strain our voices

Above a secret,

And casual, interrupted be

Our words of reminiscence

(Of no more use to us

The black going of the sun).

Little by little let's remember the past

And the stories told in the past

Now twice told

Stories that speak to us

Das flores que na nossa infância ida

Com outra consciência nós colhíamos

E sob uma outra espécie

De olhar lançado ao mundo.

E assim, Lídia, à lareira, como estando,

Deuses lares, ali na eternidade

Como quem compõe roupas

O outrora compúnhamos

Nesse desassossego que o descanso

Nos traz às vidas quando só pensamos

Naquilo que já fomos,

E há só noite lá fora.

Of the flowers we used to pick in our childhood

With a different conscience we picked

And under a different kind

Of looking at the world.

And so, Lydia, by the fire, as it were,

Home gods, there in eternity

Like someone making clothes

What we once wore

In the restlessness that rest

Brings to our lives when we only think

What we once were,

And there's only night outside.

Tornar-te-ás só quem tu sempre foste.

Tornar-te-ás só quem tu sempre foste.

O que te os deuses dão, dão no começo.

    De uma só vez o Fado

    Te dá o fado, que és um.

A pouco chega pois o esforço posto

Na medida da tua força nata —

    A pouco, se não foste

    Para mais concebido.

Contenta-te com seres quem não podes

Deixar de ser. Ainda te fica o vasto

    Céu p'ra cobrir-te, e a terra,

    Verde ou seca a seu tempo.

You'll become just who you've always been.

You'll become just who you've always been.

What the gods give you, they give you in the beginning.

    All at once, Fate

    Gives you fate, that is one.

Slowly comes the effort you put in

To the extent of your innate strength -

    Not much, if you weren't

    For more.

Be content with being who you can't

Help but be. Still there is

    The sky to cover you, and the earth,

    Green or dry in its own time.

Cada dia sem gozo não foi teu

Cada dia sem gozo não foi teu

Foi só durares nele. Quanto vivas

Sem que o gozes, não vives.

Não pesa que amas, bebas ou sorrias:

Basta o reflexo do sol ido na água

De um charco, se te é grato.

Feliz o a quem, por ter em coisas mínimas

Seu prazer posto, nenhum dia nega

A natural ventura!

Every day without enjoyment wasn't yours

Every day without enjoyment wasn't yours

You only lasted in it. How long you live

Without enjoying it, you're not living.

It doesn't matter if you love, drink or smile:

Just the reflection of the sun on the water

Of a pond, if you're grateful.

Happy is one who, for having in the smallest things

Pleasure, no day denies

Natural fate!

Negue-me tudo a sorte, menos vê-la,

Negue-me tudo a sorte, menos vê-la,

Que eu, 'stóico sem dureza,

Na sentença gravada do Destino

Quero gozar as letras.

Deny me anything, Luck

Deny me anything, Luck, but to see her,

That I, 'stoic without hardness,

In the engraved sentence of Fate

want to enjoy letters.

No breve número de doze meses

No breve número de doze meses

O ano passa, e breves são os anos,

Poucos a vida dura.

Que são doze ou sessenta na floresta

Dos números, e quanto pouco falta

Para o fim do futuro!

Dois terços já, tão rápido, do curso

Que me é imposto correr descendo, passo.

Apresso, e breve acabo.

Dado em declive deixo, e invito apresso

O moribundo passo.

In the low number of twelve months

In the low number of twelve months

The year passes, and the years are short,

Few life lasts.

What are twelve or sixty in the forest

Of numbers, and how little

To the end of the future!

Two thirds already, so fast, of the course

I'm forced to run downhill, I pass.

I hurry, and soon I'm finished.

Given a slope, I quicken the pace of

The dying step.

Quero ignorado, e calmo

Quero ignorado, e calmo

Por ignorado, e próprio

Por calmo, encher meus dias

De não querer mais deles.

Aos que a riqueza toca

O ouro irrita a pele.

Aos que a fama bafeja

Embacia-se a vida.

Aos que a felicidade

É sol, virá a noite.

Mas ao que nada espera

Tudo que vem é grato.

I want ignored, and calm

I want ignored, and calm

For ignored, and own

By calm, to fill my days

Of not wanting more of them.

To those whom wealth touches

Gold irritates the skin.

To those whom fame touches

Life becomes dull.

To those whose happiness

Is the sun, night will come.

But to those who expect nothing

Everything that comes is grateful.

Colhe o dia, porque és ele.

Uns, com os olhos postos no passado,

Veem o que não veem: outros, fitos

Os mesmos olhos no futuro, veem

O que não pode ver-se.

Por que tão longe ir pôr o que está perto —

A segurança nossa? Este é o dia,

Esta é a hora, este o momento, isto

É quem somos, e é tudo.

Perene flui a interminável hora

Que nos confessa nulos. No mesmo hausto

Em que vivemos, morreremos. Colhe

O dia, porque és ele.

Harvest the day, because you are it

Some have their eyes fixed on the past,

Seeing what they don't see: others, with

The same eyes on the future, seeing

What cannot be seen.

Why go so far to put away what is near -

Our security? This is the day,

This is the hour, this is the moment, this

Is who we are, and it's everything.

Perennial flows the endless hour

That confesses us null. In the same breath

In which we live, we will die. Harvest

The day, because you are it.

Amo o que vejo

Amo o que vejo porque deixarei

Qualquer dia de o ver.

Amo-o também porque é.

No plácido intervalo em que me sinto,

Do amar, mais que ser,

Amo o haver tudo e a mim.

Melhor me não dariam, se voltassem,

Os primitivos deuses,

Que também, nada sabem.

I love what I see

I love what I see because

Someday I won't see it any longer.

I love it too because it is.

In the placid interval in which I feel

Of love, more than being,

I love that everything and me exist.

They would not give me anything better, if back

The primitive gods,

They too know nothing.

Estás só. Ninguém o sabe.

Estás só. Ninguém o sabe. Cala e finge.

Mas finge sem fingimento.

Nada 'speres que em ti já não exista,

Cada um consigo é triste.

Tens sol se há sol, ramos se ramos buscas,

Sorte se a sorte é dada.

You are alone. Nobody knows.

You are alone. Nobody knows. Be quiet and fake.

But fake without faking.

Don't expect anything that didn't exist in you already,

In oneself one is sad,

You have sun, if there is sun, you have branches if you reach for them.

You have luck, if luck is given to you.

Tenho Mais Almas que Uma

Vivem em nós inúmeros;

Se penso ou sinto, ignoro

Quem é que pensa ou sente.

Sou somente o lugar

Onde se sente ou pensa.

Tenho mais almas que uma.

Há mais eus do que eu mesmo.

Existo todavia

Indiferente a todos.

Faço-os calar: eu falo.

I have more than one soul

In us there exist multitudes

If I think or feel, I ignore

Who is it thinking or feeling.

I am just the place

Where feeling or thinking exist.

I have more than one soul

There are more Is that I

I exist however

Regardless of all.

I make them be quiet: I speak.

Os impulsos cruzados

Do que sinto ou não sinto

Disputam em quem sou.

Ignoro-os. Nada ditam

A quem me sei: eu 'screvo.

The crossed impulses

Of what I feel and don't feel

Fight for who I am to be.

I ignore them. They have no saying.

To whom I know: I write.

Vem sentar-te comigo, Lídia, à beira do rio.

Vem sentar-te comigo, Lídia, à beira do rio.

Sossegadamente fitemos o seu curso e aprendamos

Que a vida passa, e não estamos de mãos enlaçadas.

(Enlacemos as mãos).

Depois pensemos, crianças adultas, que a vida

Passa e não fica, nada deixa e nunca regressa,

Vai para um mar muito longe, para ao pé do Fado,

Mais longe que os deuses.

Come and sit with me, Lidia, by the river.

Come and sit with me, Lidia, by the river.

Let's quietly follow its course and learn

That life passes, and we're not holding hands.

      (Let's hold hands).

Then let's think, grown-up children, that life

Passes and does not stay, leaves nothing and never returns,

It goes to a sea far away, to the foot of Fate,

      Farther than the gods.

Desenlacemos as mãos, porque não vale a pena cansarmo-nos.

Quer gozemos, quer não gozemos, passamos como o rio.

Mais vale saber passar silenciosamente

    E sem desassossegos grandes.

Sem amores, nem ódios, nem paixões que levantam a voz,

Nem invejas que dão movimento demais aos olhos,

Nem cuidados, porque se os tivesse o rio sempre correria,

    E sempre iria ter ao mar.

Amemo-nos tranquilamente, pensando que podíamos,

Se quiséssemos, trocar beijos e abraços e caricias,

Mas que mais vale estarmos sentados ao pé um do outro

    Ouvindo correr o rio e vendo-o.

Let's untie our hands, because there's no point in getting tired.

Whether we enjoy it or not, we pass like the river.

It's better to pass silently

      And without too much fuss about it.

No loves, no hates, no passions that raise the voice,

No envy that makes the eyes move too much,

No cares, because if it had them, the river would always flow,

      And it would always reach the sea.

Let's love each other quietly, thinking we could,

if we wanted to, exchange kisses and hugs and caresses,

But we might as well be sitting next to each other

      Listening to the river flow and watching it.

Colhamos flores, pega tu nelas e deixa-as

No colo, e que o seu perfume suavize o momento —

Este momento em que sossegadamente não cremos em nada,

   Pagãos inocentes da decadência.

Ao menos, se for sombra antes, lembrar-te-ás de mim depois

Sem que a minha lembrança te arda ou te fira ou te mova,

Porque nunca enlaçamos as mãos, nem nos beijamos

   Nem fomos mais do que crianças.

E se antes do que eu levares o óbolo ao barqueiro sombrio,

Eu nada terei que sofrer ao lembrar-me de ti.

Ser-me-ás suave à memória lembrando-te assim — à beira-rio,

   Pagã triste e com flores no regaço.

Let's pick flowers, you take them and leave them

On your lap, and let their scent soften the moment -

This moment when we quietly believe in nothing,

      Innocent pagans of decadence.

At least, if I turn into a shadow before, you'll remember
me afterwards

Without my memory burning you or hurting you or
moving you,

Because we never held hands or kissed

      Nor were we more than children.

And if you take the coin to the shady boatman before I
do,

I won't have to suffer remembering you.

You'll be soft in my memory remembering you like this -
by the river,

      A sad pagan with flowers in her lap

Ouvi contar que outrora, quando a Pérsia

Ouvi contar que outrora, quando a Pérsia

Tinha não sei qual guerra,

Quando a invasão ardia na Cidade

E as mulheres gritavam,

Dois jogadores de xadrez jogavam

O seu jogo contínuo.

    À sombra de ampla árvore fitavam

    O tabuleiro antigo,

    E, ao lado de cada um, esperando os seus

    Momentos mais folgados,

    Quando havia movido a pedra, e agora

    Esperava o adversário,

    Um púcaro com vinho refrescava

    Sobriamente a sua sede.

I've heard that once upon a time, when Persia

I've heard that once upon a time, when Persia

Had I don't know what war,

When the invasion burned in the city

And the women screamed,

Two chess players played

Their continuous game.

> In the shade of a large tree they gazed
>
> The ancient board,
>
> And next to each one, waiting for their
>
> More leisurely moments,
>
> When he had moved the stone, and now
>
> Was waiting for his opponent,
>
> A jar of wine refreshed
>
> His thirst soberly

Ardiam casas, saqueadas eram

As arcas e as paredes,

Violadas, as mulheres eram postas

Contra os muros caídos,

Traspassadas de lanças, as crianças

Eram sangue nas ruas...

Mas onde estavam, perto da cidade,

E longe do seu ruído,

Os jogadores de xadrez jogavam

O jogo do xadrez.

Inda que nas mensagens do ermo vento

Lhes viessem os gritos,

E, ao reflectir, soubessem desde a alma

Que por certo as mulheres

E as tenras filhas violadas eram

Nessa distância próxima,

Houses were burned down, looted

Chests and walls,

Violated, women were put

Against the fallen walls,

Pierced with spears, the children

Were bloodstains in the streets...

But where they were, close to the city,

And far from its noise,

The chess players played

The game of chess.

    Even though in the messages of the wild wind

    The cries came to them,

    And, upon reflection, knew from the soul

    That the women

    And tender daughters were raped

    In that near distance,

Inda que, no momento que o pensavam,

Uma sombra ligeira

Lhes passasse na fronte alheada e vaga,

Breve seus olhos calmos

Volviam sua atenta confiança

Ao tabuleiro velho.

Quando o rei de marfim está em perigo,

Que importa a carne e o osso

Das irmãs e das mães e das crianças?

Quando a torre não cobre

A retirada da rainha branca,

O saque pouco importa.

E quando a mão confiada leva o xeque

Ao rei do adversário,

Pouco pesa na alma que lá longe

Estejam morrendo filhos.

Even though, just as they were thinking it,

A faint shadow

Passed across their foreheads, aloof and vague,

Soon their calm eyes

Turned their attentive trust

To the old board.

When the ivory king is in danger,

What does flesh and bone matter

Of sisters and mothers and children?

When the rook doesn't cover

The retreat of the white queen,

The loot matters little.

And when the trusted hand takes the check

To the opponent's king,

It weighs little on the soul that far away

Children are dying.

Mesmo que, de repente, sobre o muro

Surja a sanhuda face

Dum guerreiro invasor, e breve deva

Em sangue ali cair

O jogador solene de xadrez,

O momento antes desse

(É ainda dado ao cálculo dum lance

Pra a efeito horas depois)

É ainda entregue ao jogo predilecto

Dos grandes indiferentes.

    Caiam cidades, sofram povos, cesse

    A liberdade e a vida,

    Os haveres tranquilos e avitos

    Ardem e que se arranquem,

    Mas quando a guerra os jogos interrompa,

    Esteja o rei sem xeque,

Even if, suddenly, over the wall

The furious face appears

Of an invading warrior, and soon

Fall there in blood

The solemn chess player,

The moment before that

(He is still given to calculating a move

To take effect hours later)

Is still given to the favorite game

Of the great indifferents.

      Fall cities, suffer peoples, cease

      Freedom and life,

      The tranquil and avid possessions

      Burn and are torn apart,

      But when war interrupts the games,

      Let the king be unchecked,

E o de marfim peão mais avançado

Pronto a comprar a torre.

    Meus irmãos em amarmos Epicuro

    E o entendermos mais

    De acordo com nós-próprios que com ele,

    Aprendamos na história

    Dos calmos jogadores de xadrez

    Como passar a vida.

Tudo o que é sério pouco nos importe,

O grave pouco pese,

O natural impulsa dos instintos

Que ceda ao inútil gozo

(Sob a sombra tranquila do arvoredo)

De jogar um bom jogo.

    O que levamos desta vida inútil

    Tanto vale se é

And the more advanced ivory pawn

Ready to swap the rook.

      My brothers in loving Epicurus

      And in understand him more

      According to ourselves rather than to him,

      Let us learn from the story

      Of the calm chess players

      How to get through life.

Les us not care much about anything serious,

Let serious things weigh little,

The natural impulse of instinct

May we give it to useless enjoyment

(Under the quiet shade of the grove)

Of playing a good game.

      What we take from this useless life

      It's worth so much

A glória; a fama, o amor, a ciência, a vida,

Como se fosse apenas

A memória de um jogo bem jogado

E uma partida ganha

A um jogador melhor.

A glória pesa como um fardo rico,

A fama como a febre,

O amor cansa, porque é a sério e busca,

A ciência nunca encontra,

E a vida passa e dói porque o conhece...

O jogo do xadrez

Prende a alma toda, mas, perdido, pouco

Pesa, pois não é nada.

Ah! sob as sombras que sem querer nos amam,

Com um púcaro de vinho

Ao lado, e atentos só à inútil faina

Glory; fame, love, science, life,

As if it were only

The memory of a game well played

And a match won

To a better player.

     Glory weighs like a rich burden,

     Fame like a fever,

     Love tires, because it is serious and searching,

     Science never finds,

     And life passes and hurts since it knows you…

The game of chess

Binds the whole soul, but, lost, it weighs little

Because it's nothing.

     Ah! under shadows that unintentionally love us,

     With a glass of wine

     by our side, and only attentive to the useless toil

Do jogo do xadrez,

Mesmo que o jogo seja apenas sonho

E não haja parceiro,

Imitemos os persas desta história,

E, enquanto lá por fora,

Ou perto ou longe, a guerra e a pátria e a vida

Chamam por nós, deixemos

Que em vão nos chamem, cada um de nós

Sob as sombras amigas

Sonhando, ele os parceiros, e o xadrez

A sua indiferença.

1-6-1916

Of the game of chess,

Even if the game is just a dream

And there is no partner,

Let's imitate the Persians of this story,

And while out there,

Near or far, war and homeland and life

Call out to us, let us

Let them call us in vain, each one of us

Under the friendly shadows

Dreaming, he, of his partners, and chess

Of its indifference.

Breve o dia, breve o ano, breve tudo.

Breve o dia, breve o ano, breve tudo.

Não tarda nada sermos.

Isto, pensando, me de a mente absorve

Todos mais pensamentos.

O mesmo breve ser da mágoa pesa-me,

Que, inda que magoa, é vida.

Short the day, short the year, short everything.

Short the day, short the year, short everything.

Shortly we are nothing..

In my mind, this thought absorbs

All the other thoughts.

If sorrow being brief weighs me down,

Which, even though it is sorrow, is life.

Mestre, são plácidas

Mestre, são plácidas

Todas as horas

Que nós perdemos.

Se no perdê-las,

Qual numa jarra,

Nós pomos flores.

Não há tristezas

Nem alegrias

Na nossa vida.

Assim saibamos,

Sábios incautos,

Não a viver,

Master, they are placid

Master, they are placid

All the hours

That we lose.

If we in losing them,

Like in a vase,

We place flowers.

There are no sorrows

Or joys

In our lives.

So let us know,

Wise fools,

Not to live it,

Mas decorrê-la,

Tranquilos, plácidos,

Tendo as crianças

Por nossas mestras,

E os olhos cheios

De Natureza...

A beira-rio,

A beira-estrada,

Conforme calha,

Sempre no mesmo

Leve descanso

De estar vivendo.

But to last,

Peaceful, placid,

With the children

As our teachers,

And our eyes full

Of nature...

By the river,

By the road,

As it comes,

Always in the same

Light rest

Of living.

O tempo passa,

Não nos diz nada.

Envelhecemos.

Saibamos, quase

Maliciosos,

Sentir-nos ir.

Não vale a pena

Fazer um gesto.

Não se resiste

Ao deus atroz

Que os próprios filhos

Devora sempre.

Time passes,

Telling us nothing.

We grow old.

Let us know, almost

Wicked,

How to feel ourselves go.

There's no point

To make a gesture.

You can't resist

The atrocious god

Who his own children

Always devours.

Colhamos flores.

Molhemos leves

As nossas mãos

Nos rios calmos,

Para aprendermos

Calma também.

Girassóis sempre

Fitando o Sol,

Da vida iremos

Tranquilos, tendo

Nem o remorso

De ter vivido.

Let's pick flowers.

Let's wet lightly

Our hands

In the calm rivers,

To learn

Calm too.

Sunflowers always

Gazing at the sun,

We'll go through life

Calm, having

Not even the regret

Of having lived.

Coroai-me de rosas,

Coroai-me de rosas,

Coroai-me em verdade

De rosas —

Rosas que se apagam

Em fronte a apagar-se

Tão cedo!

Coroai-me de rosas

E de folhas breves.

E basta.

Crown me with roses,

Crown me with roses,

Crown me in truth

With roses -

Roses that fade

On fading foreheads

So soon!

Crown me with roses

And short leaves.

And that's enough.

About the authors: Fernando Pessoa - One and Many - by ChatGPT

Fernando Pessoa, born on June 13, 1888, in Lisbon, Portugal, is one of the most enigmatic and influential figures in the world of poetry and literature. He is celebrated for his profound and introspective works, which have left a mark on the literary landscape of the 20th century.

Pessoa's early life was marked by tragedy and loss. At the age of five, he lost his father, and shortly afterward, his family relocated to Durban, South Africa. There, he received an English education, which greatly influenced his writing. Pessoa returned to Portugal in 1905, and his early works reflect the duality of his cultural influences - Portuguese and English.

One of Pessoa's most remarkable literary achievements is the creation of heteronyms, distinct literary personalities with their own styles and perspectives. These heteronyms allowed him to explore diverse themes and emotions within his poetry and prose. The most famous of these heteronyms include Alberto Caeiro, a nature-loving poet; Ricardo Reis, a stoic poet inspired by classicism; Álvaro de Campos, a modernist poet; and Bernardo Soares, the author of "The Book of Disquiet," a deeply introspective and philosophical work.

Throughout his life, Pessoa's writings delved into themes of identity, existence, and the multifaceted nature of reality. His works, often characterized by their melancholic and existential tone, resonate with readers and critics alike. His poetry is marked by its introspection and exploration of the human condition, reflecting the uncertainty and flux of modern life.

Pessoa's literary career was not limited to poetry. He was an accomplished essayist, translator, and critic, contributing significantly to Portuguese literature. Despite his literary talents, Pessoa lived a relatively reclusive life, working as a freelance translator and collaborating with various literary magazines.

Pessoa died on November 30, 1935, at the age of 47, due to cirrhosis of the liver. In death, he left behind a treasure trove of unpublished works, which continue to be discovered and published to this day.

Fernando Pessoa's legacy endures through his profound and innovative body of work, which has inspired generations of poets and writers around the world. His ability to navigate the complexities of human existence and his unique approach to literature have solidified his place as one of Portugal's most celebrated literary figures and a global literary icon.

About the Authors: Ricardo Reis

Ricardo Reis: The Stoic Poet - by ChatGPT

Ricardo Reis, one of Fernando Pessoa's most renowned heteronyms, emerges as a literary persona within the rich tapestry of Pessoa's creative world. Born in 1887 in Oporto, Portugal, Reis embodies a distinct philosophical and poetic character that sets him apart in the constellation of Pessoa's heteronyms.

Reis's poetic voice is deeply rooted in his Stoic philosophy, a belief system that prizes emotional restraint and inner tranquility. This philosophy is not merely a backdrop to his work; it is the very essence of his poetry. His verses are characterized by their formal precision, a sense of order, and a contemplative tone that contrasts starkly with the emotional turbulence found in Pessoa's other heteronyms.

Educated as a doctor, Reis moved to Brazil but later returned to Lisbon, where he lived a life of routine and detachment. His existence, much like his poetry, reflects the Stoic ideals of living in harmony with nature and accepting the impermanence of life.

Reis's poetry often explores themes of time, mortality, and the transitory nature of existence. He contemplates the passage of time with serene acceptance, viewing it as an inexorable force. This contemplation is evident in his Odes as he adopts the persona of the Roman poet Horace, infusing the work with classical elegance and stoic wisdom.

One of Reis's most famous poems, "To Be Great, Be Whole," encapsulates his Stoic philosophy, urging readers to embrace self-restraint and inner balance to achieve greatness. His verses, marked by their classical allusions and meticulous craftsmanship, evoke a sense of timeless wisdom.

Ricardo Reis's contributions to Pessoa's literary universe add a layer of complexity and depth. While Pessoa's other heteronyms often grapple with existential crises and identity, Reis stands as a serene and steadfast figure who embodies the ideals of Stoicism. His poetry, though distinct from Pessoa's own style, enriches the broader landscape of Portuguese literature and offers readers a unique perspective on life's eternal questions.

Although Pessoa and Reis exist as two distinct entities, their collaboration within the poet's mind exemplifies the boundless creativity and philosophical exploration that define Pessoa's literary legacy. Through Ricardo Reis, Pessoa invites us to contemplate the virtues of inner peace and the enduring relevance of ancient wisdom in our modern world.

About this translation

This translation is my own version of Pessoa's poems revisiting verses stuck in my memory for over 50 years - half lived in Brazil/Portuguese, half lived in the US/English. It is written for my American English children and friends.

Paraphrasing Pessoa in the closing lines of The Herd Keeper poem 8:

This is the story of my Fernando Pessoa.
Why is it that
It cannot be truer
Than whatever other translators think
And academics teach?

Erick Messias is a Brazilian American physician and translator.

Printed in Dunstable, United Kingdom